TABLE OF CONTENTS

Novel-Ties® are printed on recycled paper.

Copyright © 2010 by LEARNING LINKS

For the Teacher

This reproducible study guide to use in conjunction with the novel *Dolphins at Daybreak* consists of lessons for guided reading. Written in chapter-by-chapter format, the guide contains a synopsis, pre-reading activities, vocabulary and comprehension exercises, as well as extension activities to be used as follow-up to the novel.

In a homogeneous classroom, whole class instruction with one title is appropriate. In a heterogeneous classroom, reading groups should be formed: each group works on a different novel at its own reading level. Depending upon the length of time devoted to reading in the classroom, each novel, with its guide and accompanying lessons, may be completed in three to six weeks.

Begin using NOVEL-TIES for reading development by distributing the novel and a folder to each child. Distribute duplicated pages of the study guide for students to place in their folders. After examining the cover and glancing through the book, students can participate in several pre-reading activities. Vocabulary questions should be considered prior to reading a chapter; all other work should be done after the chapter has been read. Comprehension questions can be answered orally or in writing. The classroom teacher should determine the amount of work to be assigned, always keeping in mind that readers must be nurtured and that the ultimate goal is encouraging students' love of reading.

The benefits of using NOVEL-TIES are numerous. Students read good literature in the original, rather than in abridged or edited form. The good reading habits, formed by practice in focusing on interpretive comprehension and literary techniques, will be transferred to the books students read independently. Passive readers become active, avid readers.

SYNOPSIS

Dolphins at Daybreak is the ninth book in the *Magic Tree House* series. In this adventure, Annie and her older brother Jack meet with Morgan le Fay in their tree house to find out about their next adventure. She explains that to become Master Librarians they must solve four riddles. The first riddle is on a scroll she gives them, and to solve it she hands them a book titled *Ocean Guide*. As the siblings wish that they were at the ocean, the tree house begins to swirl.

Jack and Annie find themselves on a coral reef. They read their riddle, which asks them to find something rough and gray with great beauty hidden inside. While the children explore the interior of a mini-sub that is lying on the beach, they accidentally cause it to slide off the reef into the ocean. Inside the sub, Jack and Annie discover the underwater beauty of the coral reef. As they observe marine animals, Jack uses the *Ocean Guide* to do some research on them. Two friendly dolphins appear that Annie names Sukie and Sam. Annie begins to read the mini-sub's log. From the entries she learns that the mini-sub has some dangerous cracks in its hull and was left on the beach to await pick-up by a helicopter.

Realizing they are in danger in the damaged vessel, Jack and Annie try to surface, but a giant octopus appears, fixing its tentacles on the sub. To make matters worse, the cracks in the hull widen, allowing water to flow into the sub. Jack finally manages to get the sub to the surface but is disturbed to see a hammerhead shark swimming nearby.

With the sub filling with water, Jack and Annie must attempt to swim back to the reef even though sharks are present. The children remain calm, not wanting to splash the water and attract the sharks. Still far from the reef and exhausted, Jack and Annie get sudden help from Sukie and Sam. The gentle dolphins swim to the children's aid and carry them to the reef.

Worried that he has not solved the riddle, Jack happens to pick up an oyster. Researching it, he realizes this might be the rough gray thing with something beautiful inside—a pearl. Satisfied with this discovery, the siblings make their way back to the tree house and soon swirl home to Pennsylvania.

PRE-READING ACTIVITIES

1. Preview the book by reading the title and looking at the picture on the cover. What do you think this story will be about? Do you think the story events will be real or make-believe?

2. This is the ninth book in the *Magic Tree House* series. Have you read any other books in the series? If you have, what is the same in all of the books? What changes from one book in the series to another?

3. Read the chapter titles on the Contents page at the beginning of the book. Use clues in these titles to make predictions about what might happen in the story. After you finish the book, return to your predictions and see if any of them did happen.

4. Have you ever seen a TV show or movie that showed divers in the ocean? What equipment did the divers use? What were they looking for underwater? Tell whether you would like to dive in the ocean and why.

5. Have you ever read or seen a movie about time or space travel? Where did the people go? How did they get there? Do you think time or space travel is possible? If it were possible, where would you like to go?

6. Brainstorm with your classmates to tell what you know about each of the ocean animals in a chart, such as the one below. Write this information in the chart. As you read, add new information.

	What I Know	**What I Learned**
Giant Octopus		
Hammerhead Sharks		
Dolphins		
Oysters		

Pre-Reading Activities (cont.)

7. Look at the story map below. Fill it in as you read *Dolphins at Daybreak*. List the main events in the order that they happen.

STORY MAP

Title _____

Author _____

Main characters_____

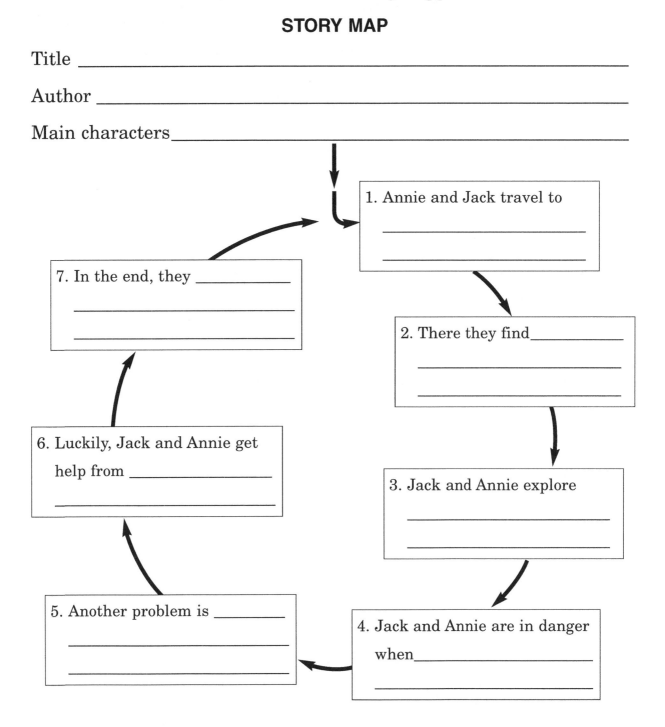

1. Annie and Jack travel to

_____

_____

2. There they find_____

_____

_____

3. Jack and Annie explore

_____

_____

4. Jack and Annie are in danger

when_____

_____

5. Another problem is _____

_____

_____

6. Luckily, Jack and Annie get

help from _____

_____

7. In the end, they _____

_____

_____

CHAPTER 1

Vocabulary: Read the words in the Word Box. Then write each word next to its clue. The letters going down in the boxes spell a word that tells what Jack and Annie are sure to have.

WORD BOX		
ancient	mysteriously	robe
librarian	research	scroll
master	riddle	velvet

1. very, very old

2. hard question to answer

3. very soft cloth

4. find out facts about a topic

5. someone in charge of many books

6. someone who is very good at doing something

7. in a strange and hard-to-know way

8. old type of book that was rolled up

9. long flowing clothing

Answer: __ __ __ __ __,__ __ __ __

Chapter 1 (cont.)

Word Study: Compound Words

A compound word is made from two smaller words

hill + side = hillside   base + ball = baseball

Draw a line from a word in column A to a word in column B to make a compound word. Then write the compound words on the lines. The words are from *Dolphins at Daybreak*.

A	B	
tree	way	1._____
back	book	2._____
note	stairs	3._____
door	pack	4._____
down	top	5._____

Read to find out why the children go back to the magic tree house.

Questions:

1. Why do both Jack and Annie want to go to the tree house on the same morning?

2. Who meets the children at the magic tree house?

3. Why does Morgan le Fay call upon the children?

4. Why does Morgan le Fay want the children to become Master Librarians?

5. What do Jack and Annie have to do to become Master Librarians?

6. What two things does Morgan le Fay give the children? Why does she give these things to them?

7. What happens after Jack and Annie make their wish?

Chapter 1 (cont.)

Questions for Discussion:

1. Why do you think Jack and Annie are eager to travel back in time again?

2. Why do you think Jack and Annie don't tell their mother where they are going?

3. What do you predict will happen next in the story?

4. What do you think Annie means when she says some dreams are real?

Literature Connection:

Morgan le Fay is gathering books for Camelot. Go online or go to the library to learn about Camelot. Do some research of your own to find out more about this kingdom. Is it a real place or make believe? Morgan le Fay also mentions that Merlin the Magician is up to his tricks again. Find out about Merlin and his mysterious powers.

Writing Activity:

Imagine you are Jack and Annie. Write a note to your parents telling them where you are going. Explain what you hope to find out.

CHAPTER 2

Vocabulary: Use the words in the Word Box and the clues below to complete this crossword puzzle.

```
                    WORD BOX
    coral      hull      mini-sub      skeleton
    hatch      lapped    reef
```

Across

3. body or frame of ship

4. hard supporting part of an animal

6. narrow ridge of rock, sand, or coral in the ocean

Down

1. stony substance secreted from the skeletons of small sea animals

2. small underwater boat

3. door to a ship

5. splashed against gently

Read to find out where the magic tree house lands.

Chapter 2 (cont.)

Questions:

1. What are the four clues in the riddle?

2. Where does the magic tree house land?

3. What strange-looking object do Jack and Annie find on the beach? Why is this object useful to oceanographers?

4. Why does Annie suggest they go inside the object?

5. According to the Ocean Guide, why does the mini-sub have a computer?

6. What happens when Annie pushes buttons on the control panel?

Questions for Discussion:

1. Can you guess what the four clues are leading the children to?

2. Why do you think it is good that Jack has the Ocean Guide?

3. Do you think Jack and Annie should have gone inside the mini-sub?

4. What do you think will happen next?

Science Connection:

In Chapter Two, Jack and Annie are on a pink coral reef. Go online or go to the library to learn about coral reefs. Fill in the chart below.

Coral Reefs	
How They Were Formed	
Where They Are Located	
Why They Are Important	

Chapter 2 (cont.)

Art Connection:

Imagine you could take a ride in a mini-sub near a reef in a tropical sea. Draw a picture of what you might see in the water around your little craft.

Writing Activity:

Jack likes to take notes about what he sees and does. Pretend you are Jack. Write some notes that sum up his adventure so far.

CHAPTERS 3, 4

Vocabulary: Read each group of words. Choose the one word in each group that does not fit with the others and cross it out. On the line below the words, tell how the rest of the words are alike.

1. computer   screen   keyboard   reef

   These words are alike because_____

   _____.

2. seagrass   jellyfish   starfish   seahorse

   These words are alike because_____

   _____.

3. mountains   flowers   caves   valleys

   These words are alike because_____

   _____.

4. smooth   rough   slippery   sleek

   These words are alike because_____

   _____.

5. dolphin   clam   stingray   shark

   These words are alike because_____

   _____.

Read to find out what Annie and Jack see under water.

Questions:

1. How do Annie and Jack steer the mini-sub?
2. What do Jack and Annie hope to find under the water?

Chapters 3, 4 (cont.)

3. Who are Sam and Sukie?
4. Why isn't a dolphin the answer to the riddle?
5. Why does Jack want to return to the beach right away?

Questions for Discussion:

1. Who seems to be more adventurous—Jack or Annie? Why do you think so?
2. Why does Jack say, "It's like we're in a fish tank"?
3. How does the ocean book help Jack and Annie on their adventure?

Science Connection:

Do some research to learn about one of the sea animals that Jack and Annie saw under water. You may want to choose a stingray, a giant clam, a seahorse, or a dolphin. Draw a detailed picture of the animal you choose. Label the different parts of the animal's body. Then write three interesting facts about the animal.

Writing Activity:

Think about what you have read so far in *Dolphins at Daybreak*. Think about the title and cover illustration of the book. Make two predictions about the adventure that Jack and Annie will soon have.

I predict that _____

_____

_____

_____.

I also predict that_____

_____

_____

_____.

CHAPTER 5

Vocabulary: Use details in each of the sentences below to figure out the meaning of the underlined word. Write your definition. Then check your definition with a dictionary.

1. Each day, the captain wrote in the ship's <u>log</u>, giving details about the trip.

   Your definition: _____

   Dictionary definition: _____

2. The <u>oceanographer</u> collected samples of sea animals and then she studied them in her lab.

   Your definition: _____

   Dictionary definition: _____

3. Our old car had a <u>defective</u> gas tank that leaked gas all over the road.

   Your definition: _____

   Dictionary definition: _____

4. We rented a truck to <u>transport</u> furniture to our new house.

   Your definition: _____

   Dictionary definition: _____

5. We all had a feeling of <u>relief</u> once we knew that the tornado was not coming our way.

   Your definition: _____

   Dictionary definition: _____

> Read to find out why the children need to leave the ocean floor in a hurry.

Chapter 5 (cont.)

Questions:

1. Why are Jack and Annie happy to be returning to the reef?

2. Why did the oceanographer leave the sub on the beach?

3. Why are the children frightened as their sub rises?

Questions for Discussion:

1. Why might the giant octopus be a problem for Jack and Annie?

2. Do you think Jack and Annie regret going out in the mini-sub?

Word Study: Prefix

If you see a word that begins with *oct*, it usually means that the word has to do with 8 things. For example, an octopus has 8 tentacles. Choose a word that starts with the prefix *oct* from the Word Box to complete each of the sentences below.

WORD BOX				
octagenarian	octagon	octave	octet	octuplets

1. A figure with <u>8</u> sides is an_____.

2. A person who has lived for <u>80</u> years is an_____.

3. <u>8</u> musicians who play music together is an_____.

4. The <u>8</u>-note musical scale is an_____.

5. <u>8</u> babies born to the same parents on the same day are_____.

Chapter 5 (cont.)

Word Study: Verbs

Verbs are words that show action. Colorful verbs help us see the action in a story.

> Jack and Annie scrambled for the hatch.

The verb in this sentence is *scrambled*. How does it help you see the action? Underline the colorful verb in each sentence below.

1. The mini-sub jerked backwards.

2. Waves lapped the shore.

3. The dolphins flipped their tails.

4. They tapped their noses against the glass.

5. Slowly, the octopus crept through the water.

Literary Element: Characterization

Jack and Annie are really different. We can see that from what they say. Read each pair of lines from the story. In the blanks, write *Jack* or *Annie* to show who was talking.

1. "I just pressed a few keys—" said _____.

   "What? I said not to touch anything!" said _____.

2. "We have to get back to the reef," said _____.

   "Oh, no, not right away," said_____. "It's so beautiful down here."

Writing Activity:

Pretend you are Jack or Annie. Write a few entries in the log of the mini-sub. Tell about your underwater adventure. Explain why you are nervous and upset now.

CHAPTER 6

Vocabulary: Draw a line from each word on the left to its meaning on the right. Then use the numbered words to fill in the blanks in the sentences below.

1. curiosity   a. dim; hard to see

2. tentacles   b. worried; troubled

3. polite   c. odd or fantastic

4. bothered   d. desire to learn or know more

5. shadowy   f. long, slender growths on the body of an animal

6. weird   g. having or showing good manners

. . . .

1. It is _____ to say "Please" and "Thank-you."

2. The octopus grabbed the fish with its eight _____.

3. The light from the lamp cast a _____ outline on the window curtain.

4. My bad grades in school always _____ Mom and Dad.

5. To satisfy my _____, I asked my parents many questions.

6. The shark's _____ head gave it the name hammerhead shark.

> Read to find out what new danger Jack and Annie face.

Questions:

1. According to the guide book, why does the octopus approach the mini-sub?

2. Why are the octopus' tentacles a problem?

Chapter 6 (cont.)

3. What do Jack and Annie suddenly notice in the ceiling of the mini-sub?

4. Why does the octopus suddenly leave in a cloud of dark ink?

5. What new danger do Jack and Annie suddenly face?

Questions for Discussion:

1. Why does Jack say they are really in trouble now?

2. Why do you think the author ends each chapter at an exciting point?

3. What do you think will happen next in the story?

Literature Study: Mood

Dolphins at Daybreak is a scary book. How does the author create the scary mood? Write a few scary details from the story. What words and phrases add to the scary mood?

_____

_____

_____

_____

Writing Activity:

Write a short paragraph to tell what you think Jack and Annie should do to escape the hammerhead shark.

CHAPTERS 7, 8

Vocabulary: Draw a line from each word on the left to its meaning on the right. Then use the numbered words to answer the questions below.

1. calm		a. move up and down with short, jerky motions
2. peer		b. peaceful; without excitement
3. fin		c. look closely at; peep
4. zigzag		d. work hard against difficulties
5. struggle		e. flow suddenly in a stream; squirt
6. bob		f. move sharply from one side to another
7. spurt		g. paddle-like part of fish used to move the fish forward, to steer, and to balance

. . . .

1. What might happen to a fish if it did not have its fins?

_____

2. When might someone want to zigzag instead of going in a straight path?

_____

3. What two things might bob along the surface of the water and not sink?

_____

4. Why might someone struggle to climb a high mountain?

_____

5. Where would you peer if you lost your keys?

_____

6. What would you do if you wanted to feel calm?

_____

7. What are two things that might spurt out of a bottle?

_____

Chapters 7, 8 (cont.)

Read to find out how Jack and Annie make it back to the reef.

Questions:

1. Why do Jack and Annie take the sub up to the top?

2. Why don't they ride the sub back to the reef?

3. Why do Jack and Annie try to stay calm in the water?

4. What does Jack see zigzagging through the water?

5. Why can't Jack and Annie swim all the way to the reef?

6. How are Jack and Annie rescued from the water?

Questions for Discussion:

1. Do you think Jack and Annie made good decisions in an emergency?

2. What do you think happened to the mini-sub?

3. Was Jack wise not to tell Annie that he saw a shark?

4. Do you think the actions of the dolphins are believable?

Science Activity:

Go online to find out more about the mini-subs and submersibles used by oceanographers. Find out the names of these vessels and how they are used. Find out how treasure hunters use mini-subs to explore the ocean around shipwrecks.

Chapters 7, 8 (cont.)

Graphic Organizer: Sequence

Jack and Annie's trip to the ocean has been full of excitement. Here are some of the things that have happened. Place the adventures in order in the boxes from 1 to 6. The first one has been done for you.

☐	meeting Sam and Sukie
☐	escaping a sinking ship
1	finding a mini-sub
☐	facing off with an octopus
☐	being chased by a shark
☐	being rescued

Writing Activity:

Write about a real or imagined time when you felt you were in danger. Tell where you were and what the danger seemed to be. Tell whether you remained calm. Then describe what you did to find your way to safety.

CHAPTERS 9, 10

Vocabulary: Synonyms are words with the same or similar meanings. Draw a line from each numbered word in column A to its synonym in column B. Then use the words in column A to fill in the blanks in the sentences below.

A	B
1. chattered	a. annoy
2. nuzzled	b. glowing
3. shallow	c. smoothly
4. blurry	d. talked
5. irritate	e. low
6. shimmering	f. kissed
7. gracefully	g. fuzzy

. . . .

1. The dancer spun _____ around the stage.

2. We waded in the _____ water of the lake.

3. The gold coins were _____ in the sunlight.

4. The birds at the feeder _____ at the big squirrel.

5. The stone in my shoe began to _____ my foot.

6. In the steamy room, my glasses became _____ and I couldn't read.

7. The mother dog _____ her young puppies with her nose.

> Read to learn whether Jack and Annie solve their riddle.

Questions:

1. How do Jack and Annie reach the reef?

2. Why do Jack and Annie think they have failed on their trip?

Chapters 9, 10 (cont.)

3. Why does Annie think she has stepped on the answer to the riddle?

4. What makes the children sure they have answered the riddle?

5. How do Jack and Annie get back to Pennsylvania?

6. What do the children still have to do to become Master Librarians?

Questions for Discussion:

1. The title of Chapter Ten is "The True Pearl." In your opinion, what is the true pearl?

2. Why is it funny when Jack and Annie tell their parents they didn't get their feet wet?

3. What did Jack and Annie learn from their adventure?

Literary Device: Simile

A simile is a comparison of two things that are not alike, using the words "like" or "as." For example:

> The sun shone on the ocean. It sparkled like a diamond.

What are the waters of the ocean being compared to?

_____

Why is this better than just saying, "The waters of the ocean shone brightly"?

_____

_____

Writing Activity:

Write a riddle like the one Morgan le Fay gave to Jack and Annie. Your riddle should be hard—but not too hard to answer. Give your riddle to a classmate and see if he or she can answer it.

CLOZE ACTIVITY

The following passage is taken from Chapter Eight of *Dolphins at Daybreak*. Read the entire passage before filling in the blanks. Then reread the passage and fill in each blank with a word that makes sense. Finally, you may compare your words with those of the author.

Jack realized the reef was farther away than he had thought. He kept swimming, but his arms and legs felt _____.[1]

Annie was struggling, too.

"Float" she said. _____.[2]

Jack and Annie turned onto their backs. _____[3] floated the way they had learned in _____[4] class.

We'll just rest a minute, _____[5] thought. *Then we'll keep going.*

But the _____[6] Jack floated, the more tired he felt. _____[7] he was too tired even to float. _____[8] started to sink.

The he felt something.

_____[9] heart stopped. Something pushed at him in _____[10] water.

It was slippery and alive.

Had _____[11] hammerhead caught up with them?

Jack shut his eyes and waited for the worst.

POST-READING ACTIVITIES

1. Return to the story map on page three of this study guide. Fill in the map with details from the story. Then compare your story map with those of your classmates.

2. Return to the *What I Know / What I Learned* chart in the Pre-Reading Activities on page two of this study guide. Fill in the facts you learned about dolphins, giant octopuses, hammerhead sharks, and oysters. Choose one of these ocean animals and write a short report about it.

3. Go to The Magic Tree House web site at *www.magictreehouse.com*. You will find interesting facts about all the *Magic Tree House* books there. There are games and puzzles too. You can also write a message to Mary Pope Osborne, the author of the books. Tell her what you liked most about *Dolphins at Daybreak*.

4. Which scene in *Dolphins at Daybreak* was most exciting? Choose a partner and act out the scene. One of you can play Jack. The other can play Annie. Read the dialogue that each character says. Act out the scene too. If you like, you can play your scene for the whole class.

5. **Art Connection:** With some classmates, paint a mural showing a coral reef from underwater. Paint in some of the ocean animals that Jack and Annie saw on their amazing trip.

6. Read another book in the *Magic Tree House* series. Compare it with *Dolphins at Daybreak*. Are Annie and Jack the main characters? What else is the same? What is different? Which book did you like better?

7. **Science Connection:** Do some research in magazines and online to find articles about dolphins. Share them with your class. Explain why you think dolphins interest people so much.

Post-Reading Activities (cont.)

8. **Literature Circle:** Have a literature circle discussion in which you tell your personal reactions to *Dolphins at Daybreak*. Here are some questions and sentence starters to help your literature circle begin a discussion.

   - Would you like to read another book in the series? Why or why not?

   - What did you like the best about this book? What did you like the least?

   - Who else would you like to read this book? Why?

   - What questions would you like to ask the author about this book?

   - I was scared when . . .

   - I would have liked to see . . .

   - I woiuld like to know more about . . .

   - I would like Jack and Annie to visit . . .

   - I wonder . . .

   - I learned that . . .

SUGGESTIONS FOR FURTHER READING

Fiction

Andrews, Jan. *Very Last First Time*. Simon & Schuster.

Carlstrom, Nancy White. *Swim the Silver Sea, Joshie Otter*. Penguin.

Hofmeyer, Dianne. *Do the Whales Still Sing?* Penguin.

Sheldon, Dyan. *The Whales' Song*. Penguin.

Woodman, Nancy. *Sea-Fari Deep*. National Geographic.

Nonfiction

Albee, Sarah. *Dolphins*. Scholastic.

Arvetis, Chris. *What Is an Ocean?* Checkerboard Press.

Baker, Lucy. *Life in the Ocean*. Scholastic.

Kindersley, Dorling. *What's Inside? Shells*. Scholastic.

Maestro, Betsy. *A Sea Full of Sharks*. Scholastic.

Sipiera, Paul P. *I Can Be an Oceanographer*. Childrens Press.

Tayntor, Elizabeth. *Dive to the Coral Reefs*. Random House.

Some Other Titles in the *Magic Tree House* series by Mary Pope Osborne

Fiction	Nonfiction Companion
* *Dinosaurs Before Dark*	*Dinosaurs*
* *Hour of the Olympics*	*Olympics of Ancient Greece*
* *The Knight at Dawn*	*Knights and Castles*
* *Mummies in the Morning*	*Mummies and Pyramids*
Pirates Past Noon	*Pirates*
Afternoon of the Amazon	*Rain Forests*
Sunset of the Sabertooth	*Sabertooths and the Ice Age*
Midnight on the Moon	*Space*
Thanksgiving on Thursday	*Pilgrims*
Twister on Tuesday	*Twister*
Tonight on the Titanic	*Titanic*

* NOVEL-TIES Study Guides are available for these titles.

ANSWER KEY

Chapter 1

Vocabulary: 1. ancient 2. riddle 3. velvet 4. research 5. librarian 6. master 7. mysteriously 8. scroll 9. robe; *Answer*–adventure

Questions: 1. Jack and Annie both want to go to the tree house on the same morning because each of them was visited by Morgan le Fay in a dream the night before. In each dream she had beckoned the children to join her at the tree house. 2. Morgan le Fay meets the children at the tree house. 3. Morgan le Fay calls upon the children because she needs their help to collect books for the Camelot library. 4. Morgan le Fay wants the children to become Master Librarians so that they can help her collect ancient books for Camelot. 5. To become Master Librarians, Jack and Annie must show that they can do research by solving four riddles. 6. Morgan le Fay gives the children a scroll with their first riddle to solve and an ocean guide book. She gives them the scroll because it contains the riddle, and the Ocean Guide to help them solve the riddle. 7. After the children make their wish, the tree house begins to spin and swirl as the children begin a new adventure.

Word Study: 1. treetop 2. backpack 3. notebook 4. doorway 5. downstairs

Chapter 2

Vocabulary: Across—3. hull 4. skeleton 6. reef; Down—1. coral 2. mini-sub 3. hatch 5. lapped

Questions: 1. The four clues are: something gray, something rough, something plain, but something beautiful inside. 2. The tree house lands on a coral reef in a tropical ocean. 3. Jack and Annie find a mini-sub on the reef. Oceanographers use it to study the ocean floor. 4. Annie, the more adventurous of the two children, is curious about the mini-sub and convinces Jack to climb inside with her to see what it is like. 5. The mini-sub has a computer that is used for navigational purposes. 6. By pushing buttons, Annie causes the mini-sub to slide into the sea and begin a descent to the ocean floor.

Chapters 3, 4

Vocabulary: 1. reef–the other words are alike because they all relate to a computer 2. seagrass–the other words are alike because they all name types of sea animals 3. flowers–the other words are alike because they all name types of land formations 4. rough–the other words are alike because they all describe a smooth surface 5. clam–the other words are alike because they all name creatures that swim in the sea

Questions: 1. Annie learns to push the arrow buttons; the right arrow makes the sub go right; the left arrow makes it go left. 2. Jack and Annie hope to find the answer to the riddle that Morgan has given them. 3. Sam and Sukie, as named by Annie, are the two dolphins that approach the mini-sub. 4. The dolphins do not solve the riddle because they are smooth, not rough, on the outside. 5. Jack thinks they should return the sub since it must belong to someone else.

Chapter 5

Vocabulary: 1. log–daily record of a ship's voyage kept by the captain 2. oceanographer–scientist who studies the sea and marine life 3. defective–faulty; broken in some way 4. transport–carry or take from one place to another 5. relief–comfort

Questions: 1. Jack and Annie are happy to be returning to the reef because they had just read in the sub's log on the computer that the craft was damaged and not seaworthy. They feel grateful to be making it back to the surface. 2. The oceanographer left the sub on the beach so a helicopter could transport it to a junkyard. 3. The children are frightened when they see the two large eyes and the eight tentacles of a giant octopus that seems to be coming after them.

Prefix: 1. octagon 2. octagenarian 3. octet 4. octave 5. octuplets

Verbs: 1. jerked 2. lapped 3. flipped 4. tapped 5. crept

Characterization: 1. Annie, Jack 2. Jack, Annie

Chapter 6

Vocabulary: 1. d 2. f 3. g 4. b 5. a 6. c; 1. polite 2. tentacles 3. shadowy 4. bothered 5. curiosity 6. weird

Questions: 1. According to the guide book, the giant octopus approaches the mini-sub because it is curious and probably wants to learn more about the mini-sub. 2. The octopus' tentacles are very strong and it would be hard to free them from the sub because of the

suction cups at the end of the tentacles. This could further damage the hull of the sub. 3. Jack and Annie notice cracks in the ceiling of the sub and water dripping. 4. The octopus leaves because one of its enemies, a hammerhead shark, is approaching. 5. Jack and Annie may have to confront the shark.

Chaptes 7, 8

Vocabulary:
1. b   2. c   3. g   4. f   5. d   6. a   7. e; Answers to the second part of the vocabulary question will vary.

Questions:
1. Jack and Annie take the sub up to the top because it is rapidly filling with water. 2. They cannot ride the sub all the way back to the reef because it dies in the water and will not move. 3. Jack and Annie try to stay calm because splashing and activity might attract sharks. 4. Jack sees the fin of a shark zigzagging in the water near them. 5. Jack and Annie cannot swim back to the reef because they are a long way off and soon may become very tired. 6. The two dolphins rescue Jack and Annie by swimming back to the reef with the children holding on to their fins.

Sequence:
2, 4, 1, 3, 5, 6

Chapters 9, 10

Vocabulary:
1. d   2. f   3. e   4. g   5. a   6. b   7. c; 1. gracefully   2. shallow   3. shimmering   4. chattered   5. irritate   6. blurry   7. nuzzled

Questions:
1. Jack and Annie reach the reef on the backs of the dolphins, Sam and Sukie. 2. Jack and Annie think they have failed because they have not answered their riddle and their ocean book is wet and difficult to use. 3. Annie thinks she has found the answer to the riddle when she steps on an oyster and notices that it is rough and gray on the outside, but contains a beautiful pearl inside. 4. Morgan le Fay makes the word oyster appear magically on the scroll to show they have found the answer to the riddle. 5. Jack and Annie get back to Pennsylvania by pointing to the picture of the Frog Creek woods in the Pennsylvania book, causing them to swirl there in the tree house. 6. Jack and Annie will still have to answer three more riddles to become Master Librarians.